BRITISH MUSLIM IDENTITY

Past, problems, prospects

T.J. Winter

MUSLIM ACADEMIC TRUST

The Muslim Academic Trust,
29 Clifton Road
London N3 2AS
United Kingdom

ISBN 10: 1-902350-06-5
ISBN 13: 978-1-902350-06-6

This article was first published in *Encounters, Journal of Inter-Cultural Perspectives* 8/i
(March 2002). Reprinted by kind permission of the Editors. The article was
first presented as a lecture given at the Royal Commonwealth Society, London,
on 30 April 1999, at the British Council conference entitled:
'Mutualities: Britain and Islam'.

Cover illustration: William Blake, *Moon-ark*. From Bryant's *Mythology* (1774-6).

Also available in this series:

Abdal Hakim Murad, *Understanding the Four Madhhabs*
Nuh Ha Mim Keller, *Evolution Theory and Islam*
Nuh Ha Mim Keller, *The Concept of Bid'a in the Islamic Shari'a*
Ibn Ḥajar al-'Asqalānī, tr. A. Murad, *Selections from the Fatḥ al-Bārī*
Paul Hardy, *Islam and the Race Question*

Designed by Abdullateef Whiteman

Printed in Turkey

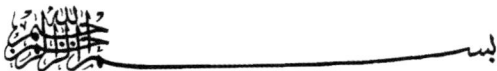

BRITISH MUSLIM IDENTITY
Past, problems, prospects

' ...following the way which is called heresy I worship the God of my fathers'.

JOHN MILTON, QUOTING ST PAUL

IN 1997 FIGURES were published which purported to show that by the year 2002 the number of regular British Muslim worshippers would outstrip the number of Christians attending Church of England services. The projection for that year was 760,000 Muslims, as compared with 756,000 Anglicans.[1] Whether or not this is a case of Disraeli's 'lies, damned lies and statistics', it is uncontroversial that Islam has become a prominent feature on Britain's religious landscape. Processes of assimilation appear to be eroding more tangential aspects of ethnic identity, but the religion itself is conforming to its usual obstinate pattern of resisting the reduction or transformation of core beliefs and practices. Put differently, there is much *bhangra* music in today's Britain, but no *bhangra* theology or worship.

Despite this, or perhaps because of it, Islam has frequently been successful in transmitting itself to the second generation. It is a success that has been complex, as many young Muslims fall away from the religion's liturgical and moral expectations, and yet this has been accompanied by the phenomenon of a discovery of urban, more nomocentric varieties of religious expression by the offspring of immigrants from rural backgrounds characterised by syncretistic forms of belief and ritual.[2] Several winds are blowing, and if mosque attendance is any sort of a guide, the community is clearly entrenching itself well.

This survival through selective transformation has combined the *ressourcement* of a distant pious past with an interaction with the ambient British culture as mediated by powerful cultural instruments such as school and the mass media. Religions exist in praxis, and despite the essentialising claims made by some preachers in the community, the closure of primary immigration ensures that British Islam is in some sense becoming more British with every passing year. The majority of U.K. Muslims are now native to this country, entailing the flourishing of English-language community newspapers, while their Urdu or Turkish equivalents one by one publish their valedictory issues. Even the pulpit, the last redoubt of the first generation's culture, is changing its nationality: mosque sermons in the East End may still be heard in Arabic, or Sylheti, but may also be delivered in faultless Estuary English.

Serious scholarship has been gearing up for at least ten years to tackle this new testing-ground for fashionable anthropological theories, and this essay will not attempt to add to that growing body of insights. Instead, some informal reflections will be offered on the larger implications of this convergence, using the framework not of the social scientist, but of the historian of religion. If we make the claim, surely a quite defensible one, that the arrival and demonstrable sustainability of a large Muslim presence in these islands is the most significant single event in our religious history since the Reformation, then we need hardly justify any attempt to ponder the ways in which the deep structures of British and Islamic identity have converged, and might converge, as the new millennium advances. The tools used to offer such an analysis can, of course, be little more than blunt instruments: one does not need to be 'religiously musical' to appreciate that the core of religious consciousness is a fugitive, ungraspable thing, and its trajectory utterly unpredictable. But there are legible texts, tendencies and habits of mind in both worlds which are now intersecting and engaging in mutual fecundation, and even though these constitute the surface rather than the quality of each narrative, they nonetheless have much to reveal. Perhaps Oscar Wilde was not being irreligious when he observed that 'it is only shallow people who do not judge by appearances'.[3]

In today's intellectual climate I need hardly remark that all conjurings with 'metanarratives', to use the loaded contemporary term, have become problematic; and that any pondering of the destiny of categories such as 'Islam' or 'British identity' must first explain its parameters. I must say that while I have much respect for the anthropological arguments of, say, Clifford Geertz, against the helpfulness of 'Islam' as an all-explicatory category on the ground, I have less patience with the more recent wave of social scientific work rooted in, or defensive of, philosophical attempts to unpick all transhistorical notions of meaning and canonicity. Deconstruction is surely itself susceptible of deconstruction in terms of the narratives it claims to supersede: Lyotard, Derrida, and the rest have something in common: they are French, and more specifically, the product of a cultural milieu that has since the *lumières* followed an increasingly sceptical, aporetic approach to knowledge, reinforced by the several calamities that have befallen French Catholicism and the nation of France itself. Perhaps postmodernism can itself be deconstructed, as the Gallic shrug turned into a worldview? In any case, its own claims to stand in judgement (for this is what it is doing) sit uneasily with its purported disclosure of the indeterminacy of all readings.

Postmodernism, a kind of Ash'arism without God, has some purchase in its exegesis of a contemporary culture which is still substantially post-war in its resistence to ideology and resolutions. Lyotard and Barthes are undeniably keen observers; yet as historical analysts their project requires an atomism that seems at odds with the evidence

3

amassed by professional historians. Most irreducibly, as Ernest Gellner saw, it conflicts with the metanarrative presented by the Islamic world.[4] Geertzian and postmodern anthropology may work as insights into the metabolism of local cultural systems; but will irretrievably break down when confronted, most conspicuously, with the curriculum and method of Sunni institutions in the diverse territories of the Islamic world. Observers allied to the postmodern turn are fascinated by particularist currents displayed by forms of folk religion, and seldom mention the mosque or the *madrasa*. The latter institutions, linked traditionally by informal networks symbolised and often energised by the Mecca pilgrimage, seem to have furnished an authentically universal dimension to Islamic culture which has trickled down via local religious personnel into the culture of the provinces. To retort that these institutions and practices could not have existed independently of the manner of their perception by human participants betrays an inability to note the startlingly effortless mutual recognition of regionally-diverse Muslim scholars at events such as the Ḥajj. The exact nature of such a recognition over the immense span of the Islamic domains may, admittedly, be elusive, not least to outsiders. Speculatively, it might be fruitful to attribute it to the rooting of the *Sharīʿa* in the body. For Maurice Merleau-Ponty, it is only the body which can liberate us from solipsism, because it provides the single universal cross-cultural field.[5] As the foundation for an authentic intersubjectivity, or 'intercorporeity', the Muslim body, the site of purity laws and the foundation of the entire nomocentric structure of Muslim discourse, appears to supply a successful basis on which to resist linguistic idealism's counter-intuitive (and utterly un-Koranic) insistence that language constitutes rather than represents reality.[6]

Geertz and postmodernist observers posit a radically disintegral *Umma*; yet a historian might see each particularity in the world-community of Islam as operative in a dynamic relationship with a measurable and more constant core grounded and experienced in the body and adumbrated in texts: the normative Sunni exegetic canon, which, far from serving as a mere site of inscription, over centuries transforms and may ultimately supplant irreconcilably pagan aspects of regional identity.

Clearly we can make a case for an Islamic metanarrative, if we define it textually in terms, most obviously, of the consensual Sunni syllabus. The standard Koranic commentaries, the manuals of *uṣūl al-fiqh* and the Ashʿarī or the Māturīdī dogmatic syntheses, and certain other texts, are remarkably uniform in their distribution over the traditional Islamic world. The religious system articulated in that canon, which seems to give more than it takes, and regularly nudges cultures in a recognisable and consistent direction, *can* be regarded as a metanarrative; whether it is the proper expression of eternal foundational propositions enshrined in the sacred texts is another matter which, for our purposes here, we need not assess.

In the United Kingdom, this metanarrative has become refocussed as well as rediversified through the process of assimilation to aspects of Britishness. The younger generation may seem more responsive to it, and to have greater access to it, than an older generation which is frequently rooted in rural particularities, and takes saintly individuals rather than texts as its source of religious authority. In some cases this disembedding may lead to a reconnection with the tradition through living Middle Eastern conservatisms, as with the *ṭarīqas* newly active in Britain;[7] in others, to a disembodying of Islam from the past and the entire rejection of sainthood in favour of texts. In both cases, however, it is clear that aspects of South Asian rustic pieties of the supernatural, even of the magical, are giving way here to various scripturalisms, both normatively traditional and Salafist. In Britain, a particularism is being universalised, and then unevenly reparticularized, entailing (and facilitated by) a shift away from Braelwi piety and towards the more mobile Shādhilī, Deobandī, Tablīghī, or Wahhābī idioms of commitment.

The other side of the equation is that of the British narrative, and, as discussions triggered by Scottish devolution have revealed, this is a no less problematic category. Popularly it is regarded as legitimate to speak of, say, 'the English', and one can still publish mass-circulation books by this title.[8] However there is a certain politically-correct, multicultural-ist tendency in the universities, and also among some social administrators, to reject as exclusionary the idea of a British metanarrative. It is not necessary, here, to challenge that interrogation directly; Britishness is certainly indefinable, and what we have traditionally taken to be its constituents are in any case today subject to rapid erosion by the same globalisation that is disembedding Islam. It seems like millennia since the days in which one could write 'Scotland is a church, not a nation' (Ernest Barker, in 1947),[9] or 'The English are a truly unified people, more unified, I would hazard, than at any previous period of their history', as the author of a newspaper survey concluded in 1951.[10] Nonetheless, the pages that follow will adhere to certain generalisations that on the whole seem easier to defend than to disprove.

The balance of this article offers two observations in connection with British receptivity to Muslimness, and with the prospects for resolving the Self-Other tension through a re-embedding of Islam in the country's sociocultural fabric. One of these must be that there are turns within traditional British religious life that can be hospitable to Islam. But first, attention must be directed to the definition of Islam as paradigmatic Other. Identities are always framed in a reflexive fashion: we are the ones who are rightly different to our neighbours. It is the contention of the next section that the British national identity differs from several of its European equivalents by lacking a history of self-construction against an Islamic rival.

★   ★   ★

In 1997 the Nobel Prize for literature went to the distinguished Portuguese writer José Saramago. One of his finest novels concerns a proof-reader in Lisbon who is asked to correct the galleys of a new standard history of his city.[11] The narrative is interwoven with glimpses of the city's most traumatic moment: its conquest, from Muslims, by a crusader army which proceeded to slaughter the population. Perhaps a hundred thousand people lost their lives in what may have been the largest single massacre of the Middle Ages. So traumatised is the proof-reader by the realisation that his beloved city took shape through ethnic cleansing, that he changes the proofs of the book as a kind of post-hoc (and postmodern) erasure of the Crusader outrage. Contemplating again the hard reality of a narrative on the galley proofs, he succumbs to the mortal temptation of his calling. Nietzsche's proof-reader had famously resisted the temptation to add the word 'Not' to the phrase, 'God is dead'. But here, where the text reads, 'The crusaders captured the city of Lisbon', he inserts the illicit negative. He cannot bear to live with such a history; and it must change. The consequent hue and cry following the publication of this edited version of the Portuguese national memory reveals, for Saramago, the difficulty of coming to terms with a national identity made warped and vehement by a seven hundred year-old event. Portugal's national epic, the *Lusiads*, is a sustained hymn to ethnic cleansing in a land where 'Righteous Heaven willed that here the struggle with the miscreant Moslem should prosper exceedingly and end with his total expulsion'.[12] The nation's identity has been shaped against an Islamic other, with the result that Portuguese imams today 'have constantly to calm down confused Muslim pupils (who were born in Portugal and are Portuguese), when they are taught in school that Muslims are the enemy of the Portuguese people.'[13]

Other European nations have also been shaped by polemic against the Muslim Other, construed as impure transgressor on Christian, European soil. The *Cantar de mío Cid*, as the first extended literary work in the Spanish language, has for centuries contributed powerfully to Spanish images of the self and of Islam,[14] to the extent that it survived secularisation and, for the greatest twentieth-century theorist of Spanish identity, Miguel de Unamuno, became a symbol of true

Spanish resistance to a rich alien elite.[15] Even in the New World, *cristianos y moros* plays are organised in village communities, and church retablos display the image of San Jaime 'Matamoros', recalling the unsettling presence of ambiguously-converted Muslim immigrants to New Spain, and also the transposition of anti-Muslim themes into the new context of war against the Indians.[16]

Other, still more troubling, instances are not far to seek. The misfortunes of Kosovar and Bosnian Muslims during the 1990s might be viewed as the culmination of a consistent, we may say the most consistent, theme in Serbian reflection on nationhood: the struggle against the dragon of Islam. Serbia's national epic is the *Mountain Wreath* of Bishop Petar Njegoš of Montenegro. Many television images of the flight of refugees from Bosnia and Kosova would have been admirably contextualised by subtitles from this great paean to anti-Muslim violence. For instance, this is how a bishop urges his flock to the Holy War:

> Strike for the Cross! strike for heroic name!
> Whoer girds on his shining arms,
> Whoer hath heart within his breast
> Strike these blasphemers of Christ's holy name!
> Baptized be they, with water or with blood!
> Hunt we now the leper from out our fold.
> Let chanted be some terror-bringing song;
> Let the true altar rise on blood-stained stone!

At one point, this episcopal diatribe is interrupted by a Muslim, who avers:

> Small enough is this our land,
> yet two faiths there still may be
> As in one bowl two soups agree,
> Let us still as brothers live.

The bishop rejects this proposal, and the poem continues:

No single seeing eye, no Muslim tongue,
escaped to tell his tale another day.
We put them all unto the sword
All those who would not be baptised,
But who paid homage to the Holy Child,
were all baptized with sign of Christian Cross,
And as brother each was hailed and greeted.
We put to fire the Muslim houses,
That there might be nor stick nor trace,
Of these true servants of the devil!
From Cetinje to Tcheklitche we hied,
There in full flight the Muslims espied;
A certain number were by us mow'd down,
And all their houses were set ablaze,
Of all their mosques, both great and small,
We left but accursed heaps,
For passing folk to cast their glance of scorn.[17]

This is Serbia's national epic, taught and venerated as such in schools in the rump Yugoslavia, to the delight of nationalists and the 'unease' of liberals.[18]

Further East, Russian and particularly Cossack tales of expansion against Muslim principalities on the Volga, in Siberia and in the Caucasus remain popular, and have figured largely in national curricula, not least because of the role of figures such Ivan IV, Orthodox warrior against the 'Hagarenes', and St Sergius of Rodonezh, the 'builder of Russia' who prayed for victory over the Tatars and whose monastery is now one of Russia's major shrines. The *Lay of Dmitry Donskoy*, one of the founding documents of Russian literature, is a neo-Byzantine rallying cry against Islam, reflecting the sense of holy confrontation that lay at the foundation of Russian national identity;[19] in tone it is not significantly different from the Vseslav epic, which contains lines such as:

9

Keep hacking old ones, little ones,
Leave none in the realm for breeding.
Leave only by selection –
Not many nor a few, seven thousand –
Darling beautiful maidens.[20]

Later, Russia was to develop an enthusiasm for the Spanish Inquisition, and import some of its attitudes and methods.[21]

For France, Braudel has located the 'choc électrique' of the battle of Poitiers, 'le vraie première croisade,'[22] as the decisive moment in the formation of French national identity. It was this, and other Carolingian moments of self-definition against Islam, most memorably represented by France's most significant national epic the *Chanson de Roland*, which led to the 'birth of Europe'.[23]

Even Germany, with no historic borders with the Islamic world, has displayed a mentality shaped by this encounter. The connection is the Teutonic Knights, who originated as a military order in Palestine. Following the loss of their castle of Starkenberg near Jerusalem in 1268, they moved to Prussia, bringing to the great German saga of the *drang nach Osten* the military technology learned in Syria, and also the attitude of crusade. The hochmeisters of the Knights referred to the pagan Prussians as the Saracens of the North; and, as Desmond Seward has shown, the systematic brutality with which the order's territories were pushed eastwards reflect the absolutist religious attitudes acquired in the hothouse atmosphere of Outremer.[24]

The revival of the *drang nach Osten* project under the Third Reich cannot be understood except against this legacy of crusading against Muslims. The symbol of the Luftwaffe was, after all, the cross of the Teutonic knights. The SS reordering of the ethnic map was inspired by romantic memories of the policy of the Knights in their own *Ordensland*, which was rooted in Crusader techniques for the management of Muslim populations. Hitler himself was, of course, no

Christian, but he was able to motivate his listeners with a Crusading, anti-Saracen rhetoric. In his speech to the Nuremberg Rally of September 1937, he 'compared the clash between the rival *Weltanschauungen* of National Socialism and Bolshevism to that between Christianity and Mohammedanism'.[25]

By contrast, the British national myth is not constituted through reference to any such historical, Armageddon-like confrontation with Islam. As Kathleen Raine has shown, the 'Matter of Britain' emerges from the Arthurian legends and the quest for the not-quite-Christian, but not-quite-pagan Holy Grail. From Malory to Walter Scott, in Purcell's *King Arthur*, in John Cowper Powys's *Porius*, in E. White's (and Britten's) *The Sword in the Stone*, and in uncounted local recitals, the Arthurian cycle has been taken as the nearest thing Britain has to a founding epic,[26] and it has little or nothing to do with war against Muslims. It is a religious story replete with an esoteric, not an identity, symbolism: the Round Table is the zodiac, and signifies the king's domain under heaven, an imagery which may be of Middle Eastern origin. There is an unmistakeable reflection of the English style of religion in the moralistic optimism of the legends, despite the tragedy of the overthrow by Mordred. Arthur does not die; he sleeps, and will return again to reestablish justice in his kingdom; he is a messianic figure, perhaps an imam in occultation, recalling Rosicrucian legends of the sleeper Christian Rosenkreutz, who may himself be ultimately of Ismaili origin.

To make this point, that British national identity has not been figured in opposition to Islam, is not to indulge in an untroubled optimism about the future of British Muslim identity and cohabitation, it is simply to suggest that a mutuality between British and Islamic narratives will not be obstructed by a core constituent of traditional national identity. British, and more particularly English, styles of xenophobia and racism were born in Stuart wars against the Irish and native American peoples, not against Islam.

Having offered some remarks about the absence of Islamophobic themes in the country's ancient stories about itself, we now need to focus on some current tensions within British Islam, to assess the prospects for an embedding of the religion in the UK's historic identity, and in particular, in its religious fabric.

Islam's substantial presence in this country has coincided with the eruption of challenges in the Muslim heartlands to traditional Sunnism. What Eamon Duffy has called the 'stripping of the altars' is now befalling Islam, to the extent that we can speak of an Islamic reformation that is now well underway. As with the reformation in the Latin West, this aims to establish the supremacy of the transcendent over the immanent. Saints' tombs are submitting to the pickaxe, while the authority of healers, mediators, talisman-salesmen and sacred brokers of all kinds is now in question in a way that even a generation ago would have been difficult to imagine. Visitors to the Algerian countryside can already note the transformation in the skyline that has been wrought. Further south, African Islam is steadily becoming Islam in Africa.[27] Ancient patterns of indigenization are giving way to what R. Robertson has called 'glocalization', the local replication of remote (in this case Arabian) norms; 'the cocoon for the traveller who needs to go abroad but does not want to leave home'.[28]

As British Muslims form part of the wider Islamic world, they are not immune to these tendencies, and it is important to grasp their implications for a convivial and integrative existence with other communities in this country. For the ulema respected by the older generation, here as overseas, Ghazālī is normative; for many of the young, he has been displaced by Ibn Taymiya. The former held a respectful view of Christians[29] and a Shāfi'ī definition of law and practice that allowed a good deal of accommodation with local custom and new practices, and guaranteed the flexibility of Muslim societal and legal convention by allowing a large role to public interest in the revision of that majority of rulings of *Shari'a* which are deduced analogically.[30] Ibn Taymiya, writing his 'war theology' in a time of intense insecurity,[31] is strenuously anti-Christian, and vehemently defends a purist vision of Islamic society against alien accretions.[32] Sociologists like to interpret the raising of tension between Muslims and Christians in, say, Indonesia, or Nazareth, or the Sudan, as the result of essentially socio-economic transformations; and yet this view is clearly inadequate. One of the great failings of Western interpretation of the Islamic world in recent years, whether based in the universities or in the chancelleries, has been the reluctance to recognise the centrality of theology to what is taking place. Few would claim that sixteenth-century German history can be grasped without a knowledge of Christian sacramental theology and ecclesiology; and yet the Islamic world is frequently discussed in crude terms of 'fundamentalists' or 'Islamists' against national secular élites. In reality, such categories tend to be highly reductionist, and have frequently misled academic, political and media analysis. The stresses are in fact triangular, not bipolar, involving mutual negotiation and rejection between Western modernity, traditional inculturated Islam, and transcendentalist Islamism.

The new transcendentalism, with its associated animosities – not merely against Christians, but against more immanentist readings of Islam, particularly Sufism with its frequent historic willingness to accept elisions with ambient cultures – is an important key to unravelling the state of Islam, British Islam not excepted. Mosque personnel among the nationalities represented in the Azhar university in Cairo return to their countries as courteous functionaries; those trained in Madina or Riyadh frequently return as polemicists. The Egyptian training takes place in a Ghazālian paradigm, in a city where an accommodation has long been reached with a Christian and a Westernising presence, as well as with popular pieties. The training in Madina or in Riyadh is derived primarily from Ibn Taymiya, and is significantly more adversarial. A radical divergence: the one Ghazālian, accommodating and forgiving, and the other rigorist in its insistence that all hybridity is transgressive.[33]

In Britain, too, the Wahhabi presence has become significant. Here the most controversial aspect of Ibn Taymiya's agenda is widely discussed. This is the doctrine of *al-walā' wa'l-barā'*: loyalty is only to the approved imam; and all man-made authority is to be repudiated. Christians and other scripturaries have no covenant of protection, *dhimma*, unless they are under such an imam.[34]

The spread of this view was brought home to the present author when he gave a class in a small mosque in Birmingham. A young Wahhabi asked the following question: 'If I am in a Muslim country, and I have the chance to kill British tourists, should I do this if there is a danger that Muslims might also be hurt?' The question of course makes no sense in traditional Sunnism; but has a real context in certain extreme constituencies of Wahhabism. The *Gamāᶜāt* who claim responsibility for attacks on tourists in Egypt are doctrinally committed Wahhabis.[35]

The *walā' wa-barā'* doctrine indicates the scale and temper of the gulf that separates the new anti-immanentism from more normative traditionalisms. An expression of the latter has been articulated in a lecture given in California by Shaykh ᶜAbdallāh bin Bayyah, one of the most distinguished Mālikī scholars of Mauritania. Bin Bayyah told his American Muslim audience that 'the relationship between the Muslims living in this land and the dominant authorities in this land is a relationship of peace and contractual agreement – of a treaty. This is a relationship of dialogue and a relationship of giving and taking [...] It is absolutely essential that you respect the laws of the land that you are living in.' The Shaykh proceeded to explain how classical *fiqh* required conviviality and respect for non-Muslim neighbours, and allowed adaptations even of fundamental religious rules, such as the timing of prayers, to facilitate the integration of Islam in society and the workplace. He continued:

We have to maintain those things that are particular to us as a community, but we also have to recognize that there are other things that are not particular to us but rather general to the human condition that we can partake in […] We have to maintain our roots. We have deep roots in our faith, but at the same time we have to be open.[36]

Traditional Sunnism's legal and theological capacity to allow conviviality and adaptation has, of course, been demonstrated in many historical contexts. From an almost unlimited list, examples might include the ancient Muslim communities in Poland and Lithuania, which became so solidly embedded in their Catholic surroundings that they could produce two of Poland's national heroes: Jalāl al-Dīn, who supported the Grand Duke against the Teutonic Knights at Tannenberg in 1421, and Aleksander Sulkiewicz (d.1916), hero of Polish independence. Islam in the region continues to manifest a retention of its doctrinal and liturgical core in tandem with large-scale adaptations to the ambient culture, as evidenced in mosque architecture, patterns of diet and attire, and the use of Polish sonorities during religious ceremonies.[37]

No less accommodating, and accommodated, have been the Muslims of China, as shown by the role played by Sayyid-i Ajall (d.1279), the Yüan governor of Yunnan, who, while personally a devout Muslim, ordered the establishment of the province's first Confucian temples, and was responsible for the definitive introduction of Chinese culture, so that he received the title 'Loyal and Compassionate' from the emperor.[38] Hui Muslims in China, recognised as adherents of one of the country's three Heavenly Religions, wore the pigtail, and could revere Confucius as a prophet,[39] practicing an Islam with a profoundly Sinicised fragrance, but without, in general, compromising the religion's core requirements as understood by the guardians of the canon. Here, as in Poland, good Muslims consistently showed themselves to be good citizens, integrating to a high degree, but almost never succumbing to assimilation. This characteristically

Muslim mode of social integration was remarkably consistent in a wide range of cultures, breaking down only when the religious Other launched policies of persecution, as with Pedro the Cruel, Ivan the Terrible, or the Manchus.

Such Muslim indigenizations were made possible both by the secure confidence of believers in their core identities, and by the sophistication of a jurisprudence which pruned and fertilized rather than supplanted, allowing the adaptation or even the adoption of local particularities on grounds of communal interest, local consensus, or their presumed pre-Muslim sacred validity.[40] While it is clearly the case that the central tenets of Muslim theology, the forms of worship, and fundamental areas of personal law, were rarely negotiated away to secure conviviality, Islam has routinely shown its ability, as a universal religion, to evolve local styles, which are not usually intermediate stages towards a full Arabness, but sustainable local Islams that hold the universal and the particular in balance. Folk Islam is not inherently transient, aberrant or counter-canonical (an *idée fixe* of some classical Orientalist thinkers who assumed the exclusive normativeness of 'High Islam'), but may more reasonably be identified as a set of localised actualisations of an intrinsic propensity of the religion to maintain a discrete and limited canon of interpretation about God's transcendence, and an almost indefinite range of local interpretations of the Koranic passages about the divine immanence. Divine transcendence is approached in convergent ways across the *Umma*; divine immanence is perceived in permanent and radical divergence. The mosque is almost always a *jāmiʻ*, but the Sufi lodge may be a *tekke*, a *dergāh*, or a *daotang*; the mosque is oriented towards Mecca, while the dynamic core of a dervish lodge may be the tomb of a saint famously rooted in local particularities. Normative Islam, that is to say Islam as most recurrently existing, is hence *both* a high textual tradition, *and* a gamut of low traditions, whose interaction is typically highly stable. Despite the suggestion of observers such as Lamin Sanneh and V.S. Naipaul that

Islam cannot adapt adequately to local particularities but must progressively eliminate them (Islam as a travelling parochialism, or even 'Arab imperialism')[41] anthropologists usually remark upon Muslim success in indigenization, through processes that are usually gentle and mutual, and may take many centuries, and which cannot be full assimilations to local essences unless we assume that a true process of indigenization must operate in only one direction. Take, for instance, the judgement of one ethnologist of South India:

> Our study, then, appears to confirm the special genius of Islam in the course of its expansion, certainly in South and South-east Asia, to adapt to the local environment and geography, in a way that does not jeopardise the purity of its core tenets, while being as flexible as possible in the peripheral areas, to accommodate those indigenous customs and traditions that do not challenge the core tenets. This may be the secret behind the success of Islam, not only in Karikal or in the Tamil country, but in the whole of South and South-east Asia.[42]

In considering the ways in which Islam might experience further inculturation in Britain, then, I assume that the the ideology of *al-walā' wa'l-barā'* will not progress here; and that some variety of discreet counter-reformation will ensure the continuation, and no doubt the adaptation, of Sunni Islam's resources for an integrated and courteous minority life.

★   ★   ★

I turn now, at last, to my main theme. I have indicated that Islamic forms of life are more flexible at the periphery than at the core, and that this has historically provided, in substantially less liberal cultures, opportunities for indigenization and a general sense of mutual flourishing. Granted that the British and Islamic narratives are both elastic, if identifiable, cultural constructs, and that the latter has shown itself capable of thoroughly embedding itself in regional alterities, what are the prospects for Islam becoming an integrated, rather than an isolated and alien, feature on the British religious landscape? I will pass in silence over more superficial accommodations, and address what I take to be the underlying issue, which is the compatibility of Islam with British styles of religious faith.

The first and most obvious observation to make is that Islam is a cognate religion to the Christianity which is at the centre of the British religious narrative. Both religions grew from the same Semitic soil, and formulated their doctrines in the language of the same Hellenistic patrimony. Aquinas could read Ghazālī's *Maqāṣid* far more easily than he could have negotiated, for instance, the Vedas. In the first period of the Christian experience of Islam there were even thinkers who regarded the new religion as a form of Christianity, albeit an aberrant one (St John of Damascus is an example[43]), and although medieval Latin Christianity seldom shared this view, the mutual inspiration of the two traditions led some twentieth-century scholars to treat Islam as a christologically-misplaced Christianity. Louis Massignon, author of by far the most capable and informed Christian meditations on Islam, went further by regarding Islam as an essentially valid, divinely-decreed dispensation, which included Christian mysteries in occluded form: the virgin birth, Christ as logos, and so on, in order to proclaim these otherwise inaccessible truths to the Semitic world.[44] More recently, Hans Küng has affirmed the legitimacy of the prophethood of Islam's founder, using biblical criteria, as part of his conviction that Islam, and also Buddhism, have providential significance as 'correctives' to Christianity.[45] Like that of many others, his inclusivist stance in effect assimilates Islam to the invisible Christian church.

Such Christian reflections on Islam suggest that the two traditions can be today, even more than they were in the high medieval period, interlocking narratives, mutually fecund although unmistakeably distinct. They also suggest that the most hopeful point of potential fecundation and convergence is in the area of Christology. Few believe that it would be right to adjust the Nicene resolutions to accommodate the preferences of other religionists, Muslim or otherwise; but the fact that for quite other reasons – philosophical and bible-critical – an essentially Socinian option has been taken up by a considerable number of theologians in the United Kingdom, suggests that the great stumbling-block between a fuller mutual recognition of Islam and Christianity is smaller than it once was. Given that a neo-Orthodox reaction (sometimes Barthian, sometimes 'radically Orthodox') is now in full spate, it is clear that Nicene orthodoxy will not imminently be dislodged here. However, the existence of this unitarian christology, as a recognisably British theological option, suggests how Islam can present itself within the spectrum of indigenously-validated beliefs. The key figure of British religious history is Jesus of Nazareth; and if there is a space in British christology which may be labelled unitarian, and an allied soteriology which can be called Pelagian, then Islam's place becomes far clearer and less problematic.

What might be the ultimate source of specifically British reflections on the sacred? Again, the Arthurian cycles are probably the most legitimate candidate, and I want now to consider them as the starting point for a vast theological trajectory that today has led to the unitarian and Pelagian strain in British religious thinking.

With Kathleen Raine we may confirm that this founding narrative of the British people is only eccentrically Christian. The quest for the Grail is not a simple allegory of Catholic eucharistic faith and trans-formation; it is mystical, in both a Celtic and a Platonic vein. The image of the perfect ruler who, in the oldest layers of the legend, invites trans-formation in his knights, not through his own self-sacrifice, but through a self-discipline in grappling with the dragon of the self, has never been susceptible to a fully-orthodox Christian reading.

It is to this archaic stratum of the British imagination that, I believe, we may usefully source the consistent, although always minoritarian, unitarian-Pelagian strand in the religious career of this country. Milton, for example, almost wrote an epic on the Arthurian theme; and although *Paradise Lost*, which he wrote instead, and which became perhaps the greatest statement of Christian belief by an Englishman, defers to the established church in form, its intent and texture are now read by scholars as vehicles for a radical Dissent. During his lifetime Milton had written a private tract against the Trinity and the atonement; and it is against this background that we can understand his insistence on the power of grace as dispensed directly by God the Father, the parable of the Prodigal Son being, in the reading of several authorities, the paradigm for his vision of salvation.[46]

The same unitarian–Pelagian mood, accompanied by Platonic ideas, was reinforced by the arrival on the British intellectual stage of Islamic figures such as Ibn Tufayl, translated by Edward Pococke, the first Laudian Professor of Arabic at Oxford. Milton himself, in his *Prolusion*, had praised the Saracens who 'enlarged their empire as much by the study of liberal culture as by force of arms.'[47] As Nabil Matar puts it, for Milton, 'the Arabs are the example to England, not just of military prowess, but of originative imagination'.[48]

This strand could only reinforce the Pelagian and neoplatonic themes which continued to attract leading religious writers and mystics, and which had gained a particular purchase in Cambridge at the hand of dons such as Everard Digby, whose *Theoria analytica* (1579) had drawn on Platonic sources to deny the essential depravity of human nature and to insist on the possibility of a saving natural knowledge. Digby's Cambridge contemporary Peter Baro (d.1596), Lady Margaret's Professor of Divinity and champion of the 'new Pelagians', was no less dissatisfied with the insistence that God's work of salvation took place exclusively through the Atonement. Inspired by his friend Antonio del Corro (d.1591), whose *Tables of God's Works* displayed 'an eloquent silence […] on the subject of the Trinity', Baro

> claims that justification in the Old Testament meant keeping God's moral law as contained in the decalogue. Rather than contrasting law and gospel as Luther, Calvin and now Chaderton had done, Baro seems to conflate

them. Justification by faith is equated with loving God and others with sincerity. It was a shocking admission.[49]

The late Elizabethan age, borrowing from Italian Platonists such as Ficino and Pico della Mirandola who were in turn indebted to Arab philosophy, witnessed hotly-contested reactions against Augustinian definitions of grace, a preoccupation with the Old Testament almost unique in Europe, and also the first stirrings of Unitarianism, a movement which seemed to find in England more fertile ground than in virtually any other European country.

In the convergence of Platonic and Arabic philosophical notions, themselves of strongly Platonic inspiration, Dissent, in its anti-sacramental aspects, gained ground, and in some cases a necessarily covert sympathy for Islam grew with it. The first significant Western advocate of Islam was Henry Stubbe, the personal physican of James I. Stubbe, who died in 1676, had been a pupil at Westminster, the first school in Britain to have included Arabic in its curriculum; a friend of Pococke, he left a manuscript under the title *An Account of the Rise and Progress of Mahometanism, with the Life of Mahomet, and a Vindication of him and his Religion from the Calumnies of the Christians.*[50] Here is an example of his prose:

> This is the sum of Mahometan Religion, on the one hand not clogging Men's Faith with the necessity of believing a number of abstruse Notions which they cannot comprehend, and which are often contrary to the dictates of Reason and common Sense; nor on the other hand loading them with the performance of many troublesome, expensive and superstitious Ceremonies, yet enjoyning a due observance of Religious Worship, as the surest Method to keep Men in the bounds of their Duty both to God and Man.[51]

Clandestinely-circulating manuscripts of the work almost certainly made an impact on later forms of Dissent. John Toland, the Unitarian controversialist, may have acquired his epithet the

'Mahometan Christian' following a reading of Stubbe's text;[52] while no fewer than three of the manuscripts found their way into the private library of the Reverend John Disney, who in the late eighteenth century shocked the established church by publicly converting to Unitarianism.[53]

In Stubbe's work we see Islam presented not as a paradigmatic Other, but as a very English kind of religion. Stubbe is spiritual, but not superstitious. He likes simplicity: the blank, Puritan wall of the mosque rather than the elaborate stone metaphors of Catholicism or of the dizzyingly high Anglicanism of Charles.[54] He is unimpressed by complex dogma.[55] He values pragmatic morality, as is shown in his utilitarian defence of polygamy. He has no time for ideas of vicarious suffering, which seem to conflict with his (again very 'English') sense of fair play. His insistence on salvation through reflection and love is close to that of his contemporary, George Herbert, whose great poem 'Love bade me welcome' bears, for one reader, 'some affinity with medieval Islamic metaphysical poetry.'[56]

Such appreciations of Socinian religion were, of course, widely shared at the time: the names of Newton, Paley and Locke spring readily to mind. In some respects, Joseph Priestley may be said to have continued the tradition in the eighteenth century. At the turn of the nineteenth, William Blake carried on with a 'Pelagian-Platonic' strand, as a figure who was inspired by the Arthurian legacy, by the Cambridge Platonists and the English commentators on Jacob Boehme, and by a critical reading of Swedenborg. Like Milton, Blake endeavoured to take the English nation as a theme for his spiritual reflections. This he did in his so-called Prophetic Books. Reviving the idiom of the Sleeping King, Blake laments the Sleep of Albion, and urges his countrymen to free themselves from Urizen, 'aged Ignorance', who is not the Christian devil, but is the mechanistic world-view of modern science, which traps humanity in a web of deterministic, despiritualising and hence dehumanising equations and machines. He hopes

That I may awake Albion from his long & cold repose,
For Bacon and Newton, sheath'd in dismal steel, their terrors hang
Like iron scourges over Albion.

The sleep of Albion, its 'sin', is apathy, a coarsening degeneration of human awareness of the subtle and numinous.[57]

As Raine observes, 'Blake nowhere writes of the Fall in terms of Christian theology through man's disobedience and sin; rather he adopts the Platonic view of the human condition as one of forgetfulness of eternal things.'[58] He knew, as did Milton, of Plato's image in Book Ten of the *Republic*, where all souls are obliged to drink from the River of Forgetfulness before they enter the world; and to the extent that they avoid drinking deeply they become creative, religious and musical souls after birth.

It is clear why Blake never went to church. He was inspired by a neo-platonising exegesis of the Bible that also, curiously but not uniquely, brings him closer to the Old Testament. His supreme achievement in the visual arts is his set of engravings of the Book of Job, several of which may be seen in the Tate Gallery. Here we see Job achieving prosperity, and also spiritual illumination, through steadfastness and self-naughting. The salvific sacrifice of Christ is nowhere in sight.[59]

All of this is clearly compatible with the way Muslims think about salvation. Blake's image of sin as sleep coheres with the famous Koranic prologue to creation, which has all humanity summoned before God to pledge a Great Covenant to him, before enfleshment in the world.[60] Islam, and particularly the Sufi tradition within it, identifies the principle of forgetfulness (*ghafla*) as the besetting problem of man. Original Sin, for the Koran, as for Blake and the English tradition which produced him, has no place in this vision of salvation history. We need to restore ourselves, with God's help; not to be 'saved' by a vicarious divine initiative.

More could be said on this theme. Blake, through the group known as the Shoreham Ancients, influenced later movements on the fringe of British religion, some of which continue today. The religious positions of Bernard Shaw and Oscar Wilde, for instance, or the crypto-Unitarian trend which was a recurrent feature of 20th century British theology, as exampled by figures such as Geoffrey Lampe of Cambridge,[61] may well justly claim this pedigree.

★   ★   ★

The time has come to offer a conclusion. I have been trespassing in several quite different subject areas, but I hope that the need for this has been clear. My point is that the current embedding of Islam in Britain may be taken, from the Islamic perspective, as another chapter in a long story of the accommodation of minoritarian Muslim communities, a process for which there is ample precedent in Islamic law and in history. The only obstacle, as I have suggested, might be the further growth of the Wahhabi perspective, with its strong resistance to substantively embedded religion.

From the British perspective, the arrival of Islam should be seen not as the intrusion of an essentially alien worldview, but as the augmentation of an already diverse religious landscape some of whose features have already been shaped by Islam in past centuries, and which, particularly in the tradition which I have broadly characterised as Pelagian and Platonic, is clearly hospitable to Islam's central concerns.

It is for Muslims in Britain to explore and publicise this connection. To further the prosperity and integration of their important community, British Muslim leaders should consider their place not merely amid the transient landscape of race relations commissions, halal meat issues, and local politics, but also amid the deep structures of national culture. Muslims here need to be geologists, recognising that the United Kingdom has produced many expressions of the religious quest among which they can feel a genuine sense of belonging, and which can remind them of the fundamental unity of humanity. For British Muslims, the past does not have to be 'another country'.

[1] Rajeet Syal and Christopher Morgan, 'Muslims Set to Outnumber Anglicans', *Sunday Times*, 11 May 1997.

[2] See, for this process, Jessica Jacobson, *Islam in Transition: Religion and identity among British Pakistani youth* (London and New York: Routledge, 1998); Jorgen Nielsen, 'Muslims in Britain: Searching for an Identity?', *New Community* 13 (1987), 384-94.

[3] *The Picture of Dorian Gray*, chapter 2.

[4] Ernest Gellner, *Postmodernism, Reason and Religion* (London: Routledge, 1992).

[5] Mary Rose Barral, *The Body in Interpersonal Relations: Merleau-Ponty* (Lanham, MD: University Press of America, 1984). Most relevant is his discussion of the body as the site of intersubjectivity rooted in a notion of the human subject as 'incarnate spirit' as opposed to the Cartesian 'soul using a body'; see p.90. This would render the body-grounded *fiqh* experience of Muslims a unifying basis for cultural commonalty.

[6] Even the claim that language constitutes reality does not preclude it from representing it. See M.J. Devaney, *'Since at least Plato ...' and Other Postmodernist Myths* (Basingstoke: Macmillan, 1997), p.4. From the Koranic perspective, of course, language is given by God, while in Genesis it is a human construction. Muslim theology would use a scripturally-rooted theistic logocentrism to resist postmodernism.

[7] Ron Geaves, *The Sufis of Britain: An Exploration of Muslim Identity* (Cardiff: Cardiff Academic Press, 2000).

[8] Jeremy Paxman, *The English: a portrait of a people* (London: Michael Joseph, 1998).

[9] Cited in Daniel Jenkins, *The British: Their Identity and their Religion* (London: SCM, 1975), p.11.

[10] Cited by Paxman, p.6.

[11] Jose Saramago, tr. Giovanni Pontiero, *The History of the Siege of Lisbon* (London: Harvill, 1996).

[12] Luis Vaz de Camoens, *The Lusiads* (Harmondsworth: Penguin, 1952), p.80 (Canto 3).

[13] Nina Clara Tiesler, 'No Bad News from the European Margin: the New Islamic Presence in Portugal', *Islam and Christian-Muslim Relations* 12 (2001), 71-91, p.83.

[14] See e.g. Bernard F. Reilly, *The Contest of Christian and Muslim Spain 1031-1157* (Cambridge, Mass., and Oxford: Blackwells, 1992), 252-3; Israel Burshatin, 'The Docile Image: The Moor as a Figure of Force, Subservience and Nobility in the Poema de mio Cid', *Kentucky Romance Quarterly* 31 (1984), 269-280; for the wider picture see Gamal Abdel-Rahman, 'La literatura espanola ante la caida de Granada (la imagen del musulmán antes y después de 1492)', in Abdeljelil Temimi (ed.), *Actes du Ve symposium*

international d'Études morisques sur le Ve centenaire de la chute de Grenade 1492-1992 (Zaghouan: Centre d'Études et de récherches ottomanes, Morisques, de Documentation et d'information, 1993), 29-55. The Cid legend also shaped perceptions in France, and inspired the first masterpiece of French Classical theatre; cf. Peter H. Nurse (ed.) *Le Cid, by Pierre Corneille; the text of the original edition (1637), edited with an introduction, notes and variants* (London: Harrap, 1978).

[15] Miguel de Unamuno, *La Enormidad de Espana: Comentarios* (Lucero, Mexico: Editorial Seneca, 1945), 92-3. For Unamuno on the cave of Don Pelayo, initiator of the *reconquista*, as the 'zero-point' of Spanish truth against the chaos of the Other, see Carlos Blanco Aguinaga, 'Unamuno's "yoísmo" and its relation to traditional Spanish individualism', in Ramón Martínez-López (ed.), *Unamuno Centennial Studies* (Austin: Department of Romance Languages, University of Texas, 1966), 45-6.

[16] Marquez de Lozoya, 'Los moriscos en América', *Archivo del Instituto de Estudios Africanos* 14 (1960), 23-27; L. Cardaillac, 'Le probleme morisque en Amérique', *Mélanges de la Casa de Velazquez* 12 (1976), 283-306; Mercedes García-Arenal, 'Moriscos and Indians: a comparative approach', in Geert Jan van Gelder and Ed de Moor (eds), *The Middle East and Europe: Encounters and Exchanges* (Amsterdam and Atlanta: Rodopi, 1992), 39-55.

[17] P. N. Njegos, tr. James W. Wiles, *The Mountain Wreath* (London: Allen and Unwin, 1930), cited in Asim Zubcevic, 'Pathology of a Literature: Some Roots of Balkan Islamophobia', *Islamica* 2.3 (1996), 78-82.

[18] Zubcevic, 82.

[19] James H. Billington, *The Icon and the Axe: An Interpretive History of Russian Culture* (London: Weidenfeld, 1966), 54. For other literature see R. Jakobson and D. Worth, *Sofonija's Tale of the Russian-Tatar Battle on the Kulikovo Field* (The Hague: Mouton, 1963); Michael Khodarkovsky, '"Ignoble Savages and Unfaithful Subjects": Constructing Non-Christian Identities in Early Modern Russia', in D.R. Brower and E.J. Lazzerini (eds), *Russia's Orient: imperial borderlands and peoples 1700-1917* (Bloomington: Indiana University Press, 1997), 9-26. For Russian Islamophobia see further Ataullah Bogdan Kopanski, 'Burden of the Third Rome: the threat of Russian Orthodox fundamentalism and Muslim Eurasia,' *Islam and Christian-Muslim Relations* 9 (1998), 193-216.

[20] Roman Jakobson and Mark Szeftel, 'The Vseslav Epos', in Roman Jakobson and Ernest J. Simmons (eds), *Russian Epic Studies* (Philadelphia: American Folklore Society, 1949), 13-86, p.49.

[21] Billington, 70. Billington suggests that the recent Russian concept of ideological purges may be traced back to the Reconquista concept of *limpieza de sangre*.

[22] This could be contested as an anachronism. Roland, like the Cid romance, is not quite Crusader literature insofar as it lacks territorial preoccupations. Cf. Bandera

Gómez, El 'Poema de Mío Cid': poesía historia, mito (Madrid: Gredos, 1969), 51; Norman Daniel, *The Arabs and Medieval Europe* (London: Longman, 1979), 81 (on El Cid): 'his motive is the honour, rather than the extension, of Christendom.'

[23] Fernand Braudel, *L'identité de la France*. Vol 2: *Les Hommes et les Choses* (Paris: Arthaud-Flammarion, 1986), 105-6. Braudel also sees the Franco-German rapprochement under the Carolingians, reinforced by the threat from the south, as a prefigurement of modern European integration, which, one could argue, has also been partly framed as a cultural exclusion of Muslim North Africa.

[24] Desmond Seward, *The Monks of War: The Military Religious Orders* (revised edition Penguin: Harmondsworth, 1995), 95-140.

[25] Norman H. Baynes (ed.), *The Speeches of Adolf Hitler, 1922-39* (2 vols, Oxford, 1942), I, 688-712; as loosely paraphrased by Alan Bullock, *Hitler, a Study in Tyranny* (revised issue Harmondsworth: Penguin, 1990), 365. The implication is presumably that Hellenistic Christianity prizes the human will, while Islam, a Semitic faith like 'Jewish' Communism, is fatalistic.

[26] Kathleen Raine, *Golgonooza: City of Imagination. Last Studies in William Blake* (Ipswich: Golgonooza, 1991), 161-4.

[27] Eva Evers Rosander and David Westerlund (eds.), *African Islam and Islam in Africa: encounters between Sufis and Islamists* (London: Hurst, 1997).

[28] R. Robertson, *Globalization: Social Theory and Global Culture* (London: Sage, 1992), 174.

[29] Tim Winter, 'The Last Trump Card: Islam and the Supersession of Other Faiths', *Studies in Interreligious Dialogue* 9 (1999), 133-155, see 149-50.

[30] Wael B. Hallaq, *A History of Islamic Legal Theories* (Cambridge: Cambridge University Press, 1997), 112-3; cf. Muhammad Hashim Kamali, *Principles of Islamic Jurisprudence* (Cambridge: Islamic Texts Society, 1991), 267-82.

[31] Johannes J.G. Jansen, *The Dual Nature of Islamic Fundamentalism* (London: Hurst, 1997), 34, 37, who shows that his hostility to the principle of 'praiseworthy innovations' (*bidʿa ḥasana*) was rooted in his nervousness about the intentions of the newly-Islamised Mongol khanate, which permitted large-scale syncretisms among its officials and soldiery.

[32] Mohammad Umar Memon, *Ibn Taimiya's struggle against popular religion: with an annotated translation of his* Kitāb iqtiḍā' aṣ-ṣirāṭ al-mustaqīm mukhālafat aṣḥāb al-jaḥīm (The Hague: Mouton, 1976).

[33] Henri Laoust, *Essai sur les doctrines sociales et politiques de Takī-d-Dīn Aḥmad b. Taimiya* (Cairo: Institut Français d'Archéologie Orientale, 1939), 522-7.

[34] Cf. for instance the work of the Saudi-trained Muhammad Saeed al-Qahtaani, *Al-Wala' wa'l-Bara' According to the Aqeedah of the Salaf* (New Delhi: Islamic Call, 1998).

[35] Mahmud A. Faksh, *The Future of Islam in the Middle East: Fundamentalism in Egypt, Algeria and Saudi Arabia* (Westport CT and London: Praeger, 1997), 52.

[36] http://sunnah.org/articles/muslims_in_nonmuslim_lands.htm

[37] György Lederer, 'Islam in Lithuania', *Central Asian Survey* 14 (1995), 425-48; P. Borawski, 'Religious tolerance and the Tatar population in the Grand Duchy of Lithuania, 16th to 18th century', *Journal, Institute of Muslim Minority Affairs* 9 (1988), 119-133; B. Szajkowski, 'The Muslim minority in Poland', in S. Vertovec and C. Peach (eds), *Islam in Europe: the politics of religion and community* (Basingstoke: Macmillan, 1997), 91-100.

[38] P.D. Buell, 'Saiyid Ajall (1211-1279)', in E. de Rachewiltz, Hok-lam Chan, Hsiao Ch'i-ch'ing, and P.W. Geier (eds), *In the service of the Khan: eminent personalities of the early Mongol-Yüan period (1200-1300)* (Wiesbaden: Otto Harrassowitz, 1993), pp.466-79.

[39] Michael Dillon, *China's Muslim Hui Community: Migration, Settlement and Sects* (Richmond: Curzon, 1999), 80; T.W. Arnold, *The Preaching of Islam: A History of the Propagation of the Muslim Faith* (reprint Lahore: Sh Muhammad Ashraf, 1979), 310-11.

[40] E.g. (for local *ijmāᶜ* as an instrument of adjustment to local cultures) Gustav von Grunebaum, 'The Problem: Unity in Diversity', in Gustav von Grunebaum (ed.), *Unity and variety in Muslim civilization* (Chicago and London: University of Chicago Press, 1955), 31; for 'the revealed laws of those who came before us', Kamali, *Principles*, 229-234.

[41] Note the Wycliffian insistence of Lamin Sanneh, 'Muhammad's Significance for Christians: Some Personal Reflections', *Studies in Interreligious Dialogue* 1/i (1991), 25-40, p.39: 'Muslims have disenfranchised the vernacular as a canonical medium, and thus suppressed a unique and indispensable source of indigenous vitality,' which would propose the existence in Islam of a problem akin to the difficulty posed to feminists by the masculinity of Christ. It is hard to see how this has in practice impoverished Muslim cultures, given the richness of Muslim sacred literatures; one thinks, for instance, of the extraordinary vitality of Persian following the conversion of the native population; or of Turkish *mevlid* recitals, where a vernacular has been utterly sacralised to a degree unfamiliar to those worshipping in modern European languages. From a Muslim viewpoint, the thesis of the literal translatability of holy writ (see T. Winter, 'Qur'an: Translations', in *Concise Encyclopedia of Language and Religion* [London: Pergamon, 2001]) appears to suffer from three drawbacks. Firstly, it opens the door to dispute, just as 'in the rights and wrongs of translation began the earliest dissensions of the Christian Church' (A.C. Partridge, *English Biblical Translation* [London: André Deutsch, 1973], 3). Secondly, it can lead to theological displacements and anachronisms, as with the recurrent de-Judaizing of the Bible by translators. Thirdly, translation for serious liturgical and doctrinal use constitutes a

process of canonical generation which requires hierarchical guardianship, a demand outside the capacity of Islam to satisfy. Partridge (p.232) concludes his own summary of the difficulty by suggesting that 'it may be that Christians need two forms of Bible: one for the scholar-historian, another for the lay reader who demands, a little irrationally, that Scripture should be available in a language that all can understand.' Islam appears to have historically negotiated this by preserving the Arabic Koran for expert study and for devotional cantillation, and by supplying translations to satisfy popular interest in the text's meaning. Proximity to the Arabic, however, and inter-linear versions, have been the norm. Cf. Walter Benjamin: 'the interlinear version of the Scriptures is the prototype or ideal of all translation' (Walter Benjamin, ed. Hannah Arendt, tr. Harry Zohn, *Illuminations* [London: Fontana, 1973], 69). Sanneh's position forms part of a current (and entirely legitimate) reaction against Belloc's insistence that 'Christianity is Europe, and Europe Christianity'; a recent trend whose future is uncertain, given the growing enthusiasm of many Third World Christians for Western culture. For the 'Arab imperialism' thesis see V.S. Naipaul, *Beyond Belief: Islamic Excursions among the Converted Peoples* (London: Little, Brown and Co, 1998).

[42] J.B.P. More, 'The Marakkayar Muslims of Karikal, South India', *Journal of Islamic Studies* 2:1 (1991), 25-44, page 44.

[43] Daniel Sahas, *John of Damascus on Islam* (Leiden, E.J. Brill, 1972), 128-9.

[44] David A. Kerr, 'The Prophethood of Muhammad', in Yvonne Yazbeck Haddad and Wadi Zaidan Haddad (eds.), *Christian-Muslim Encounters* (Gainesville etc.: University Press of Florida, 1995), 428-30.

[45] Hans Küng et al, *Christianity and the World Religions: Paths of Dialogue with Islam, Hinduism and Buddhism* (London: Collins, 1986), 24-8. In Islam's case, the corrective takes the form of a retrieval of the historical and hence Semitic Jesus. While Küng does not deny the legitimacy of Paul's hellenising strategies; he feels that Christianity has been diminished by the atrophy of the primordial monotheism upheld by James, and he is clearly in sympathy with historians such as H.-J. Schoeps, who have speculated about an Ebionite origin for Islam.

[46] Michael Bauman, *Milton's Arianism* (Frankfurt am Main: P. Lang, 1987). The basis of Milton's objection to the Trinity was that it was unscriptural, and to the Incarnation, that 'a begotten being is not God.' The latter claim, which figured in subsequent English Unitarianism, argued from the incommunicability of the divine *ousia*.

[47] Don M. Wolfe (ed.), *Complete Prose Works of John Milton* (New Haven and London: Yale University Press, 1953-1983), I, 299, cited in Nabil Matar, *Islam in Britain 1558-1685* (Cambridge: Cambridge University Press, 1998), 87.

[48] Matar, *loc cit.*

[49] Mark R. Shaw, 'William Perkins and the New Pelagians: Another look at the

Cambridge predestination controversy of the 1590's', *Westminster Theological Journal* 58 (1996), 281. For more on the rise of English hostility to the Vicarious Atonement and the Trinity, see H.J. McLachlan, *Socinianism in Seventeenth-Century England* (Oxford: Clarendon Press, 1951).

[50] See J.R. Jacob, *Henry Stubbe: radical Protestantism and the early Enlightenment* (Cambridge: Cambridge University Press, 1983); P. M. Holt, *A Seventeenth-Century Defender of Islam: Henry Stubbe and his Book (1632-76)* (London: Dr Williams's Trust, 1972).

[51] Henry Stubbe (ed. Hafiz Mahmud Khan Shairani), *An Account of the Rise and Progress of Mahometanism, with the Life of Mahomet, and a Vindication of him and his Religion from the Calumnies of the Christians* (Second edition Lahore: Orientalia, 1954), 177.

[52] Jacob, 154-7.

[53] Holt, 10.

[54] Cf. Roger Scruton on English churches: 'The architecture is noble but bare and quiet, without the lofty aspiration of the French Gothic, or the devotional intimacy of the Italian chapel'. *England: An Elegy* (London: Chatto and Windus, 2000), p.91.

[55] Cf. Mr Vincy in *Middlemarch* (chapter 13): 'I'm a plain churchman now, just as I used to be before doctrines came up.'

[56] Clifford Longley, in *The Daily Telegraph*, April 2, 1999.

[57] Raine, *Golgonooza*, 172-5.

[58] Raine, *Golgonooza*, 172-3.

[59] Kathleen Raine, *The Human Face of God: William Blake and the Book of Job* (London: Thames and Hudson, 1982).

[60] Koran 7:172; for esoteric interpretations see G. Böwering, *The Mystical Vision of Existence in Classical Islam: The Qur'ānic Hermeneutics of the Sufi Sahl At-Tustarī (d.283/896)* (Berlin and New York: Walter de Gruyter, 1980), 145-57.

[61] G.W.H. Lampe, *God as Spirit* (Oxford: Oxford University Press, 1977). For some reflections on the book see Maurice Wiles, *Faith and the Mystery of God* (London: SCM, 1982), 117-129; especially page 127, which summarises this empirically-based English unitarian impulse well: 'To insist that the trinitarian symbolism is not only a valuable guide to reflection and worship but also disclosive of the essential nature of God himself embodies a claim to knowledge about the being of God that is hard to reconcile with the experiential and experimental character of faith'. For Lampe see C.F.D. Moule (ed.), *G.W.H. Lampe: Christian, Scholar, Churchman, a Memoir by Friends* (London and Oxford: Mowbray, 1982).